WRITER'S HANDBOOK

Rigby

Table of Contents

Introduction

Questions about writing pop up all the time, and we don't always have the answers. When do I capitalize the word **mother?** What's the correct abbreviation for **ounce?** All is not lost if you don't know the answer. All you really need to know is where to look.

The Writer's Handbook is just the place to look for all kinds of answers. It covers rules for questions about spelling, capitalization, punctuation, and grammar. Think of **The Writer's Handbook** as a place to find answers.

Capitalization

Do you ever have questions about what to capitalize in your writing? If you learn the basics, you'll be more confident as a writer. Here are a few important things to remember about capitalization.

Names of People

Capitalize the names of people and the initials that stand for those names.

Christopher Columbus

Dr. Martin Luther King, Jr.

J. K. Rowling

Tip
The first letter of first, middle, and last names is always capitalized.

Words Used as Names

Capitalize words that are used as names, such as *Mother*, *Father*, *Grandma*, and *Grandpa*.

When I visit, <u>Grandpa</u> usually gives me candy. (In this case, *Grandpa* is used as a first name.)

My <u>grandpa</u> usually gives me a hug when I visit. (In this case, *grandpa* is not used as a first name.)

Titles Used with Names

Capitalize titles used with names of people.

Queen Elizabeth

President Kennedy

Mayor Lopez

Tip
Do not capitalize titles when used without a name: *the queen, the president, the mayor.*

J.K. Rowling

Abbreviations

Capitalize abbreviations of titles and organizations.

Ph.D. (Doctor of Philosophy)

NBA (National Basketball Association)

NFL (National Football League)

Proper Nouns/Proper Adjectives

Capitalize all proper nouns and proper adjectives. A proper noun is the name of a specific person, place, or thing. When a proper noun is used to describe something, it is called a proper adjective.

Proper Nouns: **New York Yankees, Michael Jordan**

Proper Adjectives: **Chicago pizza, an English garden**

Historical Information

Capitalize the names of:

Historical events: **Civil War**

Documents: **Bill of Rights**

Eras: **Middle Ages**

Organizations

Capitalize names of organizations, businesses, teams, and political groups.

Arizona Cardinals

Boy Scouts of America

Democratic Party

Republicans

Tip

Capitalize the names of companies and the official names of products. Do not capitalize a general name for a product, such as *cereal* or *shampoo*.

Geographic Names

Capitalize all of the following:

Planets: **Earth, Pluto**

Continents: **Europe, Asia**

Countries: **Japan, Norway**

Sections of the Country: **the South, the Northeast**

States: **California, Georgia**

Provinces: **Ulster, Quebec**

Cities and Counties: **New Orleans, Cook County**

Bodies of Water: **Atlantic Ocean, Irish Sea, Mississippi River**

Mountains: **Rocky Mountains, Andes, Alps**

Public Areas: **Yellowstone National Park, Lincoln Memorial**

Roads and Highways: **Frontage Road, 17th Avenue, Interstate 70**

Buildings: **Empire State Building, John Hancock Building**

Religions, Nationalities, Languages

Capitalize names of religions, nationalities, and languages.

Religions: **Christian, Muslim**

Nationalities: **Egyptian, Australian**

Languages: **Spanish, Japanese**

Titles

Capitalize the first and last word of a title. Capitalize every word in between that is not an article (*a, an, the*), a short preposition (*in, of, on,* etc.), or short conjunction (*and, or,* etc.).

Book: **My Side of the Mountain**

Movie: **From the Earth to the Moon**

Tip

Don't be fooled! Not all short words are articles, prepositions, and conjunctions. Be sure to capitalize short words such as *Red, End,* and *Not.*

First Words

Capitalize the first word of every sentence.

The movie earned 15 million dollars in its opening weekend.

Capitalize the first word of a direct quotation.

One critic said, "The movie will be a great success."

Days, Months, and Holidays

Capitalize the days of the week, months of the year, and holidays.

Days: **Monday, Friday**

Months: **January, May**

Holidays: **Easter, Passover**

Greetings and Closings of Letters

Capitalize the first letter in the greeting. Also capitalize the first letter in the closing.

Greeting: **Dear Jane,**

Closing: **Your friend,**
 Mario

TechTip

CAPS LOCK key

SHIFT + the letter key

When you are typing on a computer, use the CAPS LOCK key or the SHIFT and the letter key to capitalize a letter.

Tip

Do not capitalize names of the seasons (*winter, spring, summer, fall*) or directions (*north, south, east, west*).

Punctuation

As you write, do you ever wonder where to place a comma or when to start a new sentence? You may know many of the rules of punctuation. After all, you punctuate your speech whenever you talk to someone. Read the examples below and see just how important correct punctuation can be.

Without punctuation:

Keisha was worried about her test she had a basketball game that afternoon and the team was counting on her to play well Keisha would have to be rested calm and relaxed she would definitely have to be happy with her test score.

With punctuation:

Keisha was worried about her test. She had a basketball game that afternoon, and the team was counting on her. To play well, Keisha would have to be rested, calm, and relaxed. She would definitely have to be happy with her test score.

You can easily learn the basics of punctuation. Read on to find out more!

Periods •

Use a period to end a sentence and to mark abbreviations, initials, and decimal points.

At the End of a Sentence

Joe's birthday party lasted well past midnight.

After Abbreviations

Dr., Mrs., Mr., Ph.D., etc., vs., ex., A.M., P.M.

Use only one period when an abbreviation marks the end of a sentence.

Our teacher uses the title of Ms.

After Initials

C. S. Lewis

Booker T. Washington

As a Decimal

Don's temperature was a feverish 101.1 degrees.

Isabel was shortchanged by $1.50 at the store.

eggs , **bacon** , and **bread** •

Commas ,

Commas help the reader know where to pause. Use a comma to break up words and ideas, and to keep sentences clear. Commas are essential in the following situations:

Items in a Series

Use a comma to separate words, phrases, or clauses in a series.

Words: **My mom picked up eggs, bacon, and bread at the grocery store.**

Phrases: **Sean enjoys playing basketball, hiking in the mountains, and riding horses.**

In Dates and Addresses

Use a comma to separate items in dates and addresses.

Date: **The Declaration of Independence was signed on July 4, 1776.**

Address: **Audrey's new address is 1200 Montview Street, Denver, Colorado 80207.**

To Set Off Dialogue

Use a comma to distinguish the words of a speaker from the rest of the sentence.

The boxer Muhammad Ali said, "I am the greatest."

Do not use a comma when you are merely reporting what someone said.

Jake said the test was easy.

In Direct Address

Use a comma to separate a noun of direct address (the person to whom one is speaking) from the rest of the sentence.

Alonso, don't eat so much right before dinner!

In Letter Writing

Use a comma after the greeting and closing in friendly letters.

Greeting: **Dear Grandpa Leo,**

Closing: **With love,**

Tip

In business letters, use a *colon* (:) after the greeting.

Dear Rigby:

To Separate Adjectives

Use a comma to separate two or more adjectives if:

- you can switch the order of the adjectives and the sentence still reads clearly.

I dislike cold, runny eggs.

I dislike runny, cold eggs.

- you can put *and* between the adjectives and still have the sentence read clearly.

I dislike cold and runny eggs.

- No commas are used when the order of the adjectives *cannot* be switched.

I dislike cold scrambled eggs.

In Numbers

Use a comma in numbers of four digits or more to keep the numbers clear.

Cathy's car was still running strong after 150,000 miles.

To Set Off Interruptions

Use a comma to set off a word, phrase, or clause that interrupts the main idea of a sentence.

Cathy was, however, longing to drive a faster car.

Between Two Independent Clauses

Use a comma between two independent clauses that are joined by a coordinating conjunction.

Ming doesn't like the color blue, so she bought the purple bike.

I'm tired today, but I have no time for a nap.

To Set Off Interjections

Use a comma to separate an interjection or short exclamation from the rest of the sentence.

Whoa, slow down!

Hey, cut it out!

To Set Off Appositives

An appositive is a word or phrase that follows a noun or pronoun and explains more about it. It renames the noun or pronoun before it. Use a comma to set off the appositive.

My aunt, a bowler, takes her bowling ball on vacation.

To Set Off Long Phrases and Clauses

Use a comma to set off a long modifying phrase or clause from a clause that follows it.

<u>After standing in the lunch line for so long</u>, I was ready to eat everything on the menu.

<u>When Jorge moved to a different city</u>, he worried about making new friends.

Semicolons ;

The semicolon works both as a comma and a period. It is used:

Between Independent Clauses

Use a semicolon to join two or more independent clauses that may each stand alone as a separate sentence.

My older brother gets to stay up later than I do; I can't wait to be his age.

To Separate Phrases

Use a semicolon to separate a series of phrases that already have commas.

People everywhere should drive less; recycle cans, glass, and paper; and save energy.

Colons :

A colon introduces a list or prepares the reader for information that follows. It is also used between numbers in time.

To Introduce a List

Use a colon to introduce a list.

Dad wanted to buy a number of things at the store: milk, cheese, toothpaste, and soap.

To Introduce a Long or Important Quotation

Use a colon to introduce a long or important quotation.

The Declaration of Independence states: "We hold these truths to be self-evident, that all men are created equal, that they are endowed by their Creator with certain unalienable rights, that among these are Life, Liberty, and the pursuit of Happiness."

Between Numbers in Time

Use a colon to separate the minutes from the hour.

School starts at 8:10 A.M.

Hyphens -

A hyphen may divide or join words. It can also create new words.

To Divide a Word

Use a hyphen to divide a word when you run out of room at the end of a line. A word can be divided only between its syllables. One-syllable words can't be divided.

Spring is my favorite season because many trees blos-som at that time of year.

To Create New Words

Use a hyphen to create new words with certain prefixes and suffixes.

ex-coach, great-uncle, fat-free

Prefixes: **all, ex, great, half, self**

Suffixes: **elect, free**

Use a hyphen to join two or more words before a noun to create an adjective.

Teddy was an ill-mannered terrier.

TIPS

- A dictionary shows where to divide a word into syllables. Heavy black dots show where hyphens are needed. For example, the dictionary follows the definition of *blossom* with its syllabication, (blos•som).
- When a word contains a double consonant, the word is often split between the consonants. (but•ter, pud•dle)
- Prefixes and suffixes usually make a separate syllable. (pre•view, hope•ful)

Dashes ▬

Use a dash to show a sudden break in the sentence or to show that a speaker has been interrupted.

In a Sentence Break

Use a dash to show a sudden break in a sentence, such as a change in thought or direction.

My dad—in case you hadn't noticed—is losing his hair.

In Interrupted Speech

Use a dash to show that another person is interrupting someone's speech.

Oh, hi—no, I hadn't heard—that's great news.

Ellipses • • •

Use an ellipsis to show that words or sentences have been omitted or to show a pause in dialogue.

Tip
When you type an ellipsis, leave a space before, after, and in between each period.

To Show Omitted Words

Use an ellipsis to show that one or more words have been omitted from a quotation.

Complete quote: **"The only thing I can be sure of is that the play begins at 9 o'clock and that we'll lose our seats if we don't arrive on time."**

Shortened quote:
" . . . the play begins at 9 o'clock . . . we'll lose our seats if we don't arrive on time."

Tip
If the ellipses are at the end of a sentence, use four periods.

Pause in Dialogue

Use an ellipsis to show a pause in dialogue, or at the end where dialogue trails off.

"I'm . . . shocked!"

"I was shocked . . ."

Quotation Marks " "

Quotation marks go around the exact words of a speaker and around titles.

Direct Quotations

Use quotation marks before and after spoken words.

Patrick Henry said, "Give me liberty or give me death!"

Placement of Punctuation

Periods and commas are always placed inside quotation marks.

"Maria, don't forget to water the plants," said Mom.

Maria replied, "Please stop nagging, Mom."

A question mark or exclamation point is placed inside the quotation marks when it punctuates the sentence in the quotes.

"Maria, do you want to get your allowance this week?" asked Mom.

It is placed outside the quotation marks when it punctuates the main sentence.

Do you ever ask your parents to "Please stop nagging"?

To Punctuate Titles

Use quotation marks to punctuate titles of songs, poems, stories, essays, magazine articles, and chapters of books.

Song: **"America the Beautiful"**

Poem: **"Casey at the Bat"**

Story: **"Second-Hand Man"**

Essay: **"Mother Tongue"**

Chapter of a Book: **"Miranda's Charm"**

Article: **"The Life of a Killer Whale"**

To Punctuate Special Words

Use quotation marks around special words in a sentence.

She had a great "excuse" for not coming to the party.

" Please stop nagging. "

Question Marks **?**

A question mark shows curiosity.

Direct Question

Use a question mark at the end of a question.

How old are you?

Exclamation Points **!**

An exclamation point expresses strong emotion. It is placed after a word, phrase, or sentence.

Word: **Oh!**

Phrase: **Happy New Year!**

Sentence: **I'm so excited about summer vacation!**

Italics and Underlining

Italics and underlining are used to show titles and for emphasis. Use italics with a computer, and underline when you write by hand.

For Titles

Use italics or underlining for titles of plays, books, newspapers, magazines, movies, or CDs.

Play: *Romeo and Juliet*, **Romeo and Juliet**

Book: *Sounder*, **Sounder**

Movie: *E.T.*, **E.T.**

For Specific Words

Use italics or underlining to show emphasis in a sentence.

That is one *big* tree!

That is one <u>big</u> tree!

Parentheses **( )**

Parentheses are placed around certain words in a sentence to add information or to make an idea more clear.

To Add Information

Use parentheses to add information.

The graph (figure 3) shows the rise in accidents on scooters.

To Make an Idea More Clear

Use parentheses to make an idea more clear.

The fans were loud (shouting and stomping their feet) at the football game.

Common Abbreviations

An abbreviation is the shortened form of a word or phrase. Most abbreviations begin with a capital letter and end with a period. Here are some common abbreviations:

Mr., Mrs., Ms., Dr., M.D., B.C., A.D., A.M., P.M.

These are acceptable in all types of writing.

Tip

In formal writing, do not abbreviate the names of states, countries, months, days, or units of measure.

Other forms of abbreviations are:

Acronyms

An acronym is a word that is formed from the first letter or letters of words in a phrase. Acronyms do not use periods.

NASA (National Aeronautics and Space Administration)

DARE (Drug Abuse Resistance Education)

SCUBA (Self-Contained Underwater Breathing Apparatus)

Initialisms

An initialism is different from an acronym. Initialisms are not pronounced as words but as separate letters.

POW (Prisoner of War)

FBI (Federal Bureau of Investigation)

TV (television)

State Abbreviations

Alabama	AL
Alaska	AK
Arizona	AZ
Arkansas	AR
California	CA
Colorado	CO
Connecticut	CT
Delaware	DE
District of Columbia	DC
Florida	FL
Georgia	GA
Hawaii	HI
Idaho	ID
Illinois	IL
Indiana	IN
Iowa	IA
Kansas	KS
Kentucky	KY
Louisiana	LA
Maine	ME
Maryland	MD
Massachusetts	MA
Michigan	MI
Minnesota	MN
Mississippi	MS
Missouri	MO

Montana	MT
Nebraska	NE
Nevada	NV
New Hampshire	NH
New Jersey	NJ
New Mexico	NM
New York	NY
North Carolina	NC
North Dakota	ND
Ohio	OH
Oklahoma	OK
Oregon	OR
Pennsylvania	PA
Rhode Island	RI
South Carolina	SC
South Dakota	SD
Tennessee	TN
Texas	TX
Utah	UT
Vermont	VT
Virginia	VA
Washington	WA
West Virginia	WV
Wisconsin	WI
Wyoming	WY

Address Abbreviations

Apartment	Apt.
Avenue	Ave.
Boulevard	Blvd.
Court	Ct.
Drive	Dr.
East	E.
Expressway	Expwy.
Heights	Hts.
Highway	Hwy.
Lake	L.
Lane	Ln.

North	N.
Park	Pk.
Parkway	Pkwy.
Place	Pl.
Road	Rd.
Rural	R.
South	S.
Square	Sq.
Station	Sta.
Street	St.
Terrace	Ter.
Turnpike	Tnpk.
West	W.

Weights and Measures

teaspoon	tsp
tablespoon	T
ounce	oz
cup	C
pint	pt
milliliter	ml
liter	L
quart	qt
gallon	gal.
millimeter	mm
centimeter	cm
meter	m
inch	in.
foot	ft
yard	yd
milligram	mg
gram	g
kilogram	kg
pound	lb
mile	mi
kilometer	km
Celsius	C
Fahrenheit	F

Contractions and Apostrophes

Many people use contractions such as *I'm* instead of *I am*, or *don't* instead of *do not*. A contraction is the shortened form of two words. An apostrophe shows where one or more letters are missing. It is quite common to use contractions in both writing and speaking. Before learning about contractions, you need to know about apostrophes.

Apostrophes

An apostrophe forms plurals, shows that one or more letters have been omitted from a word, or shows possession.

To Form Plurals

Do not use an apostrophe to create the plural of a letter, number, or sign.

Letter: **Bs**

Number: **3s**

Year: **1930s**

In Contractions

Use an apostrophe to show that one or more letters are missing.

she'd = she would, she had

I'm = I am

you're = you are

don't = do not

they'll = they will

o'clock = of the clock

In Singular Possessives

Use an apostrophe and *s* to form the singular possessive.

My <u>cousin's</u> skateboard is missing a wheel.

When the possessive has one syllable and ends in an *s* or *z* sound, add an apostrophe and *s*.

<u>Tess's</u> favorite movies are comedies.

When the possessive has two syllables and ends in an *s* or *z* sound, just add an apostrophe.

<u>Spyros'</u> parents are from Greece.

In Plural Possessives

Use an apostrophe to form the possessive of a plural noun ending in *s*.

The <u>boys'</u> bathroom is off limits.

Plural nouns not ending in *s* require an apostrophe and *s*.

The <u>women's</u> bathroom is open.

In Shared Possessives

When more than one noun shares possession, add an apostrophe and *s* to the last noun.

<u>Rosa and Carla's</u> project fell into a mud puddle.

They'll

Parts of Speech

Our language is like a spider's web. Spiders know exactly how to weave long-lasting and beautiful webs. To ensure a web's strength, spiders carefully link many different threads. In language, we link different types of words to create strong sentences. Just as webs blow away without their connecting threads, language falls apart without the correct parts of speech. By studying the parts of speech, you can learn how to weave words into strong and beautiful sentences.

Nouns

A noun names a person, place, thing, or idea.

Persons: **Nathan, mother, plumber**

Places: **Idaho, grocery store, front yard**

Things: **ball, candy, toolbox**

Ideas: **anger, shyness, nervousness**

Common and Proper Nouns

A common noun names a general person, place, thing, or idea. Common nouns begin with lowercase letters.

man, dog, singer, river, country

A proper noun names a specific person, place, thing, or idea. It is always capitalized.

Sammy Sosa, Black Labrador, Nile River, Ireland

Concrete and Abstract Nouns

A concrete noun names something that may be touched or seen.

book, bed, car

An abstract noun names something that cannot be touched or seen.

love, pain, joy, imagination

Singular and Plural Nouns

A singular noun names only one person, place, thing, or idea.

friend, lake, pencil, fear

A plural noun names more than one person, place, thing, or idea.

friends, lakes, pencils, fears

Sheila (proper noun)

loves (verb)

juicy (adjective)

Uses of Nouns

Nouns may be used as subjects, predicates, or possessives.

A subject noun either does something or is the thing being referred to.

Sophia made dinner for Elena. (*Sophia* is the subject because she did something: *made dinner.*)

Dinner was prepared on time. (*Dinner* is the subject because it is the thing being referred to.)

A predicate noun renames the subject. It connects to the subject with a linking verb.

Dinner was <u>lasagna</u>. (The noun *lasagna* renames the subject *dinner.* It is linked by the verb *was.*)

A possessive noun shows possession or ownership.

Sophia made the lasagna using <u>Cynthia's</u> recipe. (The *'s* added to *Cynthia* shows that the recipe belongs to her.)

Nouns as Objects

Nouns may be direct objects, indirect objects, or the objects of a preposition.

A noun is a direct object when it receives the action of the verb.

Sophia made Elena <u>dinner</u>. (*Dinner* is the direct object because it is the thing being made.)

A noun is an indirect object when it names the person to or for whom something is being done.

Sophia made <u>Elena</u> dinner. (*Elena* is the indirect object because dinner was being made for her.)

A noun is an object of a preposition when it is part of a prepositional phrase.

Sophia made dinner using the ingredients <u>from Cynthia's</u> <u>recipe</u>. (The noun *recipe* is the object. The preposition is *from.* The prepositional phrase is *from Cynthia's recipe.*)

apples. (noun)

Pronouns

A pronoun replaces a noun. The most common pronouns are called personal pronouns.

Juan fell off the ladder.

He fell off the ladder.

Uses of Personal Pronouns

Personal pronouns include subject pronouns, object pronouns, and possessive pronouns.

A subject pronoun is the subject of a sentence.

Singular: **I like all of the boys at school.**

Plural: **They make me laugh.**

Singular: **I, you, he, she, it**

Plural: **we, you, they**

An object pronoun is used after an action verb or in a prepositional phrase.

I chased them. (*Them* comes after the action verb *chased*.)

I ran after them on the playground. (*Them* is the object in the prepositional phrase *after them*.)

A possessive pronoun shows possession or ownership.

Owen ate all of his lunch.
(*His* comes before the noun *lunch*.)

The food was mine.
(*Mine* may stand alone.)

Pronouns that come before a noun: **my, your, his, her, its, our, their**

Pronouns that stand alone: **mine, yours, his, hers, its, ours, theirs**

Tip
The form of the pronouns in your sentences must agree with the words they replace.

Eva had a lot of free time after she gave up piano lessons.
(The pronoun *she* and the word it replaces, *Eva*, agree because they are both singular.)

Eva's sisters were still very busy because they continued to take piano lessons. (The pronoun *they* and the word it replaces, *sisters*, agree because they are both plural.)

First-, Second-, and Third-Person Pronouns

These pronouns indicate whether the speaker is speaking, listening, or being spoken about.

A first-person pronoun replaces the name or names of a speaker.

<u>I</u> enjoy watching movies.
(*I* replaces the speaker's name.)

<u>We</u> enjoy watching movies at the theater. (*We* replaces the names of two or more speakers.)

A second-person pronoun replaces the name of the person or thing being spoken to.

Jennifer, do <u>you</u> want to see a movie tonight? (*You* replaces the name *Jennifer*, the person being spoken to.)

If you <u>boys</u> are going, <u>you</u> will have to buy the tickets. (*You* replaces *boys*.)

A third-person pronoun replaces the name of the person or thing being discussed.

<u>Kevin</u> said <u>he</u> would only watch an action movie. (*He* replaces *Kevin*, the person being discussed.)

The <u>boys</u> said <u>they</u> wouldn't pay for the tickets. (*They* replaces *boys*, who are the people being discussed.)

Verbs

A verb shows action or connects the subject to another word in the sentence. Verbs can be action, linking, or helping verbs.

Verbs take on many different forms. They can be singular or plural, active or passive, regular or irregular.

In addition to the present, past, and future tenses of verbs, there are special tenses of verbs called present perfect, past perfect, and future perfect.

Action Verbs

An action verb shows what the subject is doing. It makes the writing more clear.

Lina <u>jogs</u> a lot.

She <u>watches</u> cross-country races on TV.

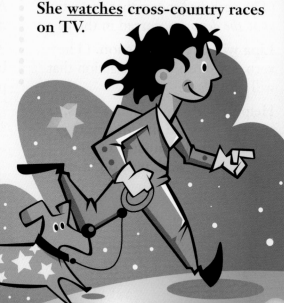

Linking Verbs

A linking verb links a subject to a noun or an adjective in the predicate part of the sentence.

Jane is an athlete. (The verb *is* connects the subject *Jane* to the noun *athlete.*)

She feels tired after a long run. (The verb *feels* links the subject *she* to the adjective *tired.*)

Verbs for states of being:
is, are, was, were, am, been

Other linking verbs: **feel, look, seem, smell, taste, turn, etc.**

Helping Verbs

A helping verb comes before the main verb in a sentence. It helps show action and time.

Lina had to go to the dentist. (The verb *had* shows that the action *go to the dentist* occurred in the past.)

Lina will get braces soon. (The verb *will* shows a future action that will take place.)

Helping verbs: **am, is, are, was, were, will, shall, been, could, would, should, must, can, may, might, have, had, has, do, did**

Singular and Plural Verbs

Use a singular verb when the subject of a sentence is singular.

Harry loves banana nut bread. (The subject *Harry* and the verb *loves* are both singular.)

Use a plural verb when the subject of the sentence is plural.

Nuts make the bread more filling. (The subject *nuts* and the verb *make* are both plural.)

Active and Passive Voice

A verb is in the active voice when the subject is doing the action in the sentence.

Rory sang the "National Anthem." (The verb *sang* is active because the subject *Rory* is doing the action.)

A verb is passive when the subject does not do the action.

The "National Anthem" was sung by Rory. (The verb *was sung* is passive because the subject, the *"National Anthem,"* is not doing the action.)

may *did*

Regular Verbs

Most verbs are regular. By adding -ed to the end of a regular verb, you show that it happened in the past. By using a helping verb, you state a past, present, or future action.

Regular Verbs:

Past	Present	Future
I baked. I have baked.	I bake.	I will bake.
He jogged. He has jogged.	He jogs.	He will jog.

Irregular Verbs

Some verbs are irregular. An irregular verb does not end in -ed when you state a past action or when you use a helping verb with it.

Irregular Verbs:

Past	Present	Future
I ran. I have run.	I run.	I will run.
She swam. She has swum.	She swims.	She will swim.

Some irregular verbs are listed below. The tense used with the helping verbs *has*, *have*, *had* is called the *past participle*.

Irregular Verbs

Present Tense	Past Tense	Past Participle	Present Tense	Past Tense	Past Participle
am, be	was, were	been	let	let	let
begin	began	begun	lie	lay	lain
bite	bit	bitten	lose	lost	lost
blow	blew	blown	make	made	made
break	broke	broken	put	put	put
bring	brought	brought	ride	rode	ridden
burst	burst	burst	ring	rang	rung
catch	caught	caught	rise	rose	risen
come	came	come	run	ran	run
cost	cost	cost	say	said	said
cut	cut	cut	see	saw	seen
dive	dove, dived	dived	set	set	set
do	did	done	shake	shook	shaken
draw	drew	drawn	shine	shone	shone
drink	drank	drunk	shrink	shrank	shrunk
drive	drove	driven	shut	shut	shut
eat	ate	eaten	sing	sang	sung
fall	fell	fallen	sink	sank	sunk
fight	fought	fought	sit	sat	sat
fly	flew	flown	speak	spoke	spoken
freeze	froze	frozen	spring	sprang	sprung
get	got	gotten	steal	stole	stolen
give	gave	given	swim	swam	swum
go	went	gone	swing	swung	swung
grow	grew	grown	take	took	taken
hang	hung	hung	teach	taught	taught
hide	hid	hidden, hid	tear	tore	torn
hit	hit	hit	throw	threw	thrown
hurt	hurt	hurt	wake	woke, waked	woken, awakened
know	knew	known			
lay	laid	laid	wear	wore	worn
lead	led	led	weave	wove	woven
			write	wrote	written

Verb Tense

The time in which the verb shows action is called tense. Tense is shown by endings (*walk**ed***) and by helping verbs (*will walk*), or by both (*will have walk**ed***).

The present tense shows an action that is happening now or that happens often.

Akemi <u>likes</u> the flute.

She <u>plays</u> often.

The past tense shows an action that happened at a certain time in the past.

Akemi <u>liked</u> the flute.

She <u>played</u> often.

The future tense shows an action that will happen later. Use such helping verbs as *will* or *shall* before the main verb.

Akemi <u>will like</u> the concert again next year.

She <u>shall play</u> the flute often.

The present perfect tense shows an action that is still happening. Use *has* or *have* before the main verb to form the present perfect tense.

Tim <u>has juggled</u> the oranges for an hour.

The past perfect tense shows an action that began and was finished in the past. Use *had* before the main verb to form the past perfect tense.

Jessica <u>had juggled</u> the oranges for 10 minutes.

The future perfect tense shows an action that will begin in the future and end at a certain time in the future. Use *will have* or *shall have* to form the future perfect tense.

Anna <u>will have juggled</u> the oranges for two hours.

Adjectives

An adjective is a word that describes a noun or pronoun. The different forms of adjectives are positive, comparative, and superlative.

> ### Tip
> Articles like *a, the,* and *an* are adjectives.

Positive Adjectives

A positive adjective describes a noun without comparing it to anything or anyone.

An elephant is <u>big</u>.

Special positive adjectives: **good, bad, many**

Comparative Adjectives

A comparative adjective compares two people, places, things, or ideas.

An elephant is <u>bigger</u> than a lion. (The ending -*er* is added to one-syllable adjectives.)

An elephant is <u>more forgetful</u> than a mouse. (You usually add *more* before an adjective with two or more syllables.)

Special comparative adjectives: **better, worse, more, less**

Superlative Adjectives

A superlative adjective compares three or more people, places, things, or ideas.

An elephant is the <u>biggest</u> animal I've seen at the zoo. (Add the ending -*est* to one-syllable adjectives.)

A lion is the <u>most frightening</u> animal I've seen at the zoo. (You usually add *most* before an adjective with two or more syllables.)

Special superlative adjectives: **best, worst, most, least**

Adverbs

An adverb describes a verb, adjective, or another adverb. Most adverbs show where, when, or how. As with adjectives, adverbs can be positive, comparative, or superlative.

Positive Adverbs

A positive adverb does not make a comparison.

Miguel works <u>hard</u> all day long.

Special positive adverbs: **well, badly, poorly**

Comparative Adverbs

A comparative adverb is formed by adding -*er* to one-syllable adverbs, or by adding the word *more* or *less* before longer adverbs.

Miguel works <u>harder</u> than other kids his age.

Miguel works <u>more often</u> than many of his friends.

Special comparative adverbs: **better, worse, less**

Superlative Adverbs

A superlative adverb is formed by adding *-est* to one-syllable adverbs, or by using the word *most* or *least* before longer adverbs.

Miguel works <u>hardest</u> in the morning.

Miguel works <u>most often</u> at his desk.

Special superlative adverbs:
best, worst, least

Tip

Be sure to use *good* and *well* correctly. *Good* is an adjective and *well* is most often an adverb. For example:
I had a <u>good</u> day because I felt <u>well</u>.

Prepositions

A preposition shows the relation of a noun or pronoun to another word in the sentence.

The puppy carelessly pushed the clock <u>off</u> the table.

The rabbit was startled and jumped <u>in</u> its cage.

Object of the Preposition

The noun or pronoun that comes after the preposition is the object of the preposition.

The cat hid <u>under</u> the <u>table</u>.
(*Table* is the object of the preposition *under*.)

Prepositional Phrases

A prepositional phrase contains a preposition, the object of the preposition, and all descriptive words in between.

The boa constrictor slithered <u>around the leg of the chair</u>.

29

Common Prepositions

about	into
above	like
across	near
after	next to
against	of
along	off
among	on
around	on top of
at	onto
before	out of
behind	outside
below	over
beneath	past
beside	since
between	through
by	to
down	toward
during	under
except	underneath
for	until
from	up
in	upon
in front of	with
inside	within
instead of	without

Interjections

An interjection expresses strong emotion or surprise. Use a comma or exclamation point to separate an interjection from the rest of a sentence.

<u>Hey</u>, stop whining!

<u>Ouch</u>! I stubbed my toe!

Conjunctions

A conjunction joins individual words or groups of words. The three types of conjunctions are coordinate, correlative, or subordinate.

Coordinate Conjunctions

A coordinate conjunction connects equal parts: two or more words, phrases, or clauses.

The snake slithered around the tree branch <u>and</u> down the trunk. (The conjunction *and* joins two prepositional phrases.)

Coordinate conjunctions:
and, but, or, nor, for, so, yet

Correlative Conjunctions

Use a correlative conjunction in pairs.

<u>Either</u> come <u>or</u> go, but make a decision. (*Either* and *or* work as a pair in this sentence.)

Correlative conjunctions:
either/or, neither/nor, both/and, not only/but, not only/also, whether/or

Subordinate Conjunctions

Use a subordinate conjunction to join two clauses to make a complex sentence.

I had to finish my math homework <u>before I was allowed to go outside and play</u>.

I'm good with numbers, <u>so I finished my homework without a problem</u>.

Subordinate conjunctions:
after, although, as if, because, before, if, in order that, since, so, that, though, unless, until, when, where, while

Writing Numbers

There are a few ways to write numbers. Here are some tips to remember when you write them:

Usually, numbers from one to nine are written as words. Numbers greater than 10 are usually written as numerals.

two, five, 12, 699, 10,000

When you compare numbers, use all numbers or all words.

The toys are popular among kids, ages 7 to 13.

Use a combination of words and numbers for very large numbers.

6 trillion, 30 million

Use words to begin a sentence.

Twenty students tried out for the play, but only six got parts.

Use numerals for numbers in the following forms:

money $4.50

decimals 10.5

percentages . . . 5%

chapters . . . . . . Chapter 1

pages . . . . page 33

addresses . . . . . 6235 W. Locust

dates . . . . October 12

times . . . . 2:00 P.M.

statistics . . . . . . a ratio of 3 to 1

Words That Add Spark to Your Writing

It's important that your writing be interesting to you and your readers. One way to add spark to your writing is to use different types of words. Antonyms, synonyms, and homonyms will not only make your writing come alive but also give you a better understanding of the words you use.

Antonyms

An antonym is a word with an opposite meaning. Antonyms create contrast and conflict in writing. The opening of Charles Dickens' *A Tale of Two Cities* is famous for its many antonyms. The words set the stage for the conflict to come.

"It was the <u>best</u> of times, it was the <u>worst</u> of times, it was the age of <u>wisdom</u>, it was the age of <u>foolishness</u> . . ."

Synonyms

A synonym is a word with a similar meaning. Synonyms enliven your writing and give the reader more than one way to think about your description.

I was <u>thrilled</u> to learn the <u>joyous</u> news that our neighbor had just won the lottery and would <u>happily</u> share his winnings with our family.

Homonyms

Homonyms are two words that sound the same but have different meanings.

Homophones are words that sound alike but have different spellings and different meanings.

The <u>witch</u> liked to <u>sail</u> through the air on her broom, <u>which</u> she had bought at a garage <u>sale</u> for a good price.

Homographs are words that have the same spellings but have different origins and meanings.

My brother needs to learn to play <u>fair</u>.

I have tickets for the <u>fair</u> this weekend.

Sentences

A sentence begins with a capital letter, includes one or more words, and ends with a period, question mark, or exclamation point. It may ask a question, make a statement, give a command, or show strong emotion, but a sentence must always express a complete thought. The main parts of a sentence are the subject, predicate, modifier, and clause. There are different kinds of sentences: simple, compound, and complex, as well as declarative, interrogative, imperative, and exclamatory. Read on to become familiar with these kinds of sentences. Then learn how to avoid making mistakes with the words, *which*, *that*, and *what*.

subject

clause

modifier

predicate

Subjects

A simple subject is the noun in a sentence that performs an action.

My neighbor <u>Kyle</u> mowed the lawn. (*Kyle* is the simple subject.)

A complete subject is the simple subject and all of the words that describe it.

<u>My neighbor Kyle</u> mowed the lawn. (*My neighbor Kyle* is the complete subject.)

A compound subject is made up of two or more simple subjects.

<u>Kyle</u> and his <u>dad</u> enjoyed a big breakfast together.

Predicates

A simple predicate is the verb that tells something about the subject.

Kyle <u>mowed</u> the lawn early in the morning. (*Mowed* tells what the subject did.)

A complete predicate is the simple predicate and all of the words that describe it.

Kyle <u>mowed the lawn early in the morning</u>. (The complete predicate is *mowed the lawn early in the morning*.)

A compound predicate is made up of two or more simple predicates.

Kyle <u>set</u> the table and <u>poured</u> the juice.

Modifiers

A modifier is a word or group of words that add detail to the sentence. A modifier can be an adjective or an adverb.

Kyle mowed the lawn <u>quickly</u> and <u>evenly</u>. (*Quickly* and *evenly* are adverbs that describe in detail how Kyle mowed the lawn.)

Types of Sentences

A simple sentence expresses one complete thought. It only has one independent clause, but it may have a compound subject or a compound predicate and one or two phrases.

My back hurts. (simple sentence)

I hurt my <u>shoulders</u> and <u>back muscles</u> playing baseball.

(This simple sentence includes a compound subject, *shoulders* and *back muscles*.)

They <u>feel</u> tight and <u>will be</u> sore for a while.

(This simple sentence includes a compound predicate, *feel* and *will be*.)

My <u>shoulders</u> and <u>back muscles</u> <u>feel</u> tight and <u>are</u> sore.
(This simple sentence includes both a compound subject, *shoulders* and *back muscles*, and a compound predicate, *feel* and *are*.)

A compound sentence is made up of two or more simple sentences that are linked by a comma and a connecting word or conjunction, such as *and*, *but*, *so*, or by a semicolon.

I have read about Africa, <u>but</u> I have never been there.

I am interested in foreign countries; I hope to travel when I'm older.

A complex sentence has one independent clause and one or more dependent clauses.

<u>Although Africa is thousands of miles away</u>, I'm willing to make the long trip.
(*Although Africa is thousands of miles away* is a dependent clause. *I'm willing to make the long trip* stands alone as a sentence.)

A declarative sentence makes a statement.

Japan is an island.

An interrogative sentence asks a question.

Did you know that Tokyo is the capital of Japan?

An imperative sentence gives a command.

Take a passport if you visit Japan.

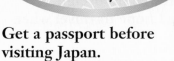

Get a passport before visiting Japan.

An exclamatory sentence shows emotion or surprise.

I'm so excited about traveling to Asia!

Clauses

A clause is a group of related words that includes a subject and a predicate.

An independent clause shows a complete thought and may stand alone as a sentence.

They wear helmets.

A dependent clause does not show a complete thought and may not stand alone as a sentence.

when <u>they</u> ride their bikes

Phrases

A phrase is a group of related words that has neither a subject nor a predicate. Phrases are not sentences. They do not form a complete thought.

The fourth-grade class (noun phrase)

acted in a play (verb phrase)

about the signing of the Declaration of Independence (prepositional phrase)

Which vs. That

Writers are often unsure when to use the words which and that. Both words add information and detail to sentences. The trick is to figure out if the information is essential to the sentence. Follow these rules to help you use the words correctly.

Use *which* to introduce a nonessential clause—information that is not essential to the sentence. Remember to use a comma to separate the added information from the main part of the sentence.

Our neighbor's house, <u>which</u> looks like a gingerbread house, is 75 years old.

Use *that* to introduce an essential clause—information that is essential to the sentence. No comma is necessary when using the word *that*.

The house <u>that</u> looks like a gingerbread house was built 75 years ago.

Which vs. What

Which is used when something can be counted, and *what* is used when something cannot be counted.

Francesca couldn't decide <u>which</u> skirt to buy. (In this case, Francesca must choose among more than one skirt.)

Francesca often has difficulty deciding <u>what</u> to buy. (In this case, it's impossible to determine how many things Francesca has difficulty deciding to buy.)

Paragraphs

Think of a paragraph as a human body, in which the brain is in control. In a paragraph, the topic sentence is like the brain. It sets the direction of the entire paragraph. The rest of the sentences are like the parts of the body. They follow the direction of the topic sentence by adding the details and examples that make the paragraph work.

A paragraph consists of the topic sentence, the body, and the closing sentence.

Topic Sentence

The topic sentence is usually the first sentence in a paragraph. It tells the reader what the paragraph will be about. A topic sentence includes a specific *topic* and *focus*.

The topic must be simple enough for a brief paragraph. A paragraph on the history of the United States, for example, would be too large a topic. A paragraph on the history of the Washington Monument, however, would work.

Too large: a paragraph on pasta
Just right: a paragraph on spaghetti

Too large: a paragraph on rivers
Just right: a paragraph on the Mississippi River

Topic sentence

Body

The focus is the specific information you want to provide about the topic. For example, a paragraph on the history of the Washington Monument might focus on the materials used to build the monument.

Topic: a paragraph on Labrador Retrievers
Focus: a paragraph on Labradors hunting ducks

Topic: a paragraph on the Mississippi River
Focus: a paragraph on how river barges on the Mississippi are used to transport goods to Illinois

Body

The body is the middle part of a paragraph. It is made up of the sentences between the topic sentence and the closing sentence. These sentences give the reader additional information about the topic.

Closing Sentence

The closing sentence ends the paragraph. It sums up the information in the paragraph and explains what it all means.

Read the following paragraph about eating spaghetti, and see how it is divided into a clear beginning, middle, and end.

Eating spaghetti is fun but a little dangerous. The dangerous part is when the food on your fork falls off. This happens to me all the time—then, plop! The meatball falls into my lap and the spaghetti goes on my shirt and makes a big red spot from the sauce. But the fun part of eating spaghetti is the sound and taste. The slurping sound is a little rude, but it reminds me how much I love spaghetti. The long, thin noodles taste good, and my grandma's special red sauce makes them even better. For me, spaghetti is the perfect meal, even if it is messy.

Closing sentence

Types of Paragraphs

The four most common types of paragraphs are descriptive, narrative, persuasive, and expository.

Descriptive Paragraphs

A descriptive paragraph describes a person, place, thing, or idea. Use words that help the reader see, hear, smell, taste, and feel what you are writing about. It's important to describe color, size, and sound. The reader should feel as though he or she is with you.

The kitchen is the best room in my house. It's always warm and inviting. I gather there with my family and friends to eat and talk about the day. I especially love the kitchen around dinnertime, when the smells of spices and cooking meat float through the air. The clanging sounds of plates and silverware remind me that I'll soon fill my stomach with delicious, homemade food.

Narrative Paragraphs

A narrative paragraph tells a story about a particular experience. The reader should feel drawn into your story and interested in what you'll describe next. Be sure to use descriptive words and details to make the experience seem more real.

I woke up early on Saturday morning to the sound of my alarm clock buzzing in my ear. I immediately hopped out of bed, threw on some clothes, and laced up my soccer shoes as quickly as I could. I dashed outside in time to see the sun rise. I had no time to waste. I began to practice right away. An hour had passed before I felt good about my dribbling and control of the ball. Another hour went by before I felt satisfied with my left-footed kick. By noon, I was drenched in sweat, sunburned, and sore all over. It was then that I knew I was ready for the game the next day.

What is the focus of this narrative paragraph? Read to find out.

Persuasive Paragraphs

A persuasive paragraph tells the writer's opinion about a topic. It also tries to convince the reader of the writer's point of view. In a persuasive paragraph, give facts and examples to help prove that your opinion is correct. The more examples you give, the more likely you are to persuade the reader.

Two annual holidays in this country are Mother's Day and Father's Day. Twice a year kids have a chance to let their parents know how much they mean to them. So it's only fair that kids get a special holiday, too. Kids need to know how much their parents care about *them*. There should be cards that say, "Happy Kid's Day!" Kids should get the day off from school to celebrate their special day, and parents should do whatever their kids want them to on that day. Kid's Day would definitely be the most popular holiday of the year!

Expository Paragraphs

An expository paragraph gives information about a topic. It explains things, gives directions, or describes how to do something. It's important to use transition words in an expository paragraph, such as *first*, *second*, *finally*, and *however*. These words make the paragraph flow more smoothly and help the reader understand the explanation.

The secret to making good pizza is using only the best ingredients. First, you have to start by making your own pizza dough. It's easy once you learn how to knead the dough and stretch it out. Next, you get the cheeses you want to put on. Make sure you have two or three kinds of really good cheese. Then get the toppings ready. I like mushrooms, onions, and green peppers on my pizza. Chop the toppings into small pieces. Then, pour the sauce over the pizza dough and spread the cheeses and toppings over the pizza. At last you are ready to bake. Your delicious pizza is only 20 minutes away.

Basic Spelling Rules

Learning to spell is like learning to play a new game. Once you learn the basic rules, you'll always remember them. Keep in mind that there are always exceptions to the rules, so it's a good idea to check a dictionary if you're unsure. Here are some tips to help you become a better speller:

i Before e

For words spelled with an *i* and *e* together, remember the phrase, "*i* before *e*, except after *c*."

receive, believe

The last part of that rule is: "except for words that sound like *weigh* and *neigh*."

sleigh, neighbor

Silent e

If a word ends with a silent *e*, drop the *e* before adding a suffix (ending) that begins with a vowel.

use	using	usable
believe	believing	believable
shake	shaking	shakable

Tip
Do not drop the e when the suffix begins with a consonant (*-ful, -ness*). For example: hopeful, shameful, sameness, bareness

Consonant Ending

If a one-syllable word with a short vowel needs an ending like *-ed* or *-ing*, double the final consonant.

mat	matted
set	setting

Words Ending in y

For plurals of words that end in *y*, change the *y* to an *i* and add *-es*. If the word ends in *ey*, add an *s*.

country	countries
monkey	monkeys

Would you like a piece of pie?

Neigh!

More Spelling Tips

Make a Dictionary

It may be helpful to keep a notebook with the words you have trouble spelling. When you see an unfamiliar word in something you are reading, look closely at the word, say the word, and write it in your notebook. You can create your own dictionary by alphabetizing the words you've written down. By writing the words and organizing them alphabetically, you'll have an easier time remembering how to spell them in the future.

Read from Bottom to Top

After you write, reread your work from bottom to top. This will help you focus on each word you have written and allow you to catch errors.

Tip

Another helpful strategy is to hold an index card under each line. This will help you focus on each line without being distracted by the other lines on the page.

Mark Unfamiliar Words

Circle or underline the words that are difficult for you. After you write, return to the words you have marked and look them up in a dictionary—maybe the one you created!

Tip

Ask a friend, family member, or teacher to read your writing. Someone who hasn't read your work yet may catch mistakes you haven't noticed.

Basic Writing Rules

Writing is your chance to let your imagination run free and express your feelings. It is a fun and rewarding process that allows you to think more deeply about many topics. As a writer, you can always change your style, use different words, and experiment with new topics. You never stop learning how to write. Here are a few basic rules to help you develop your writing:

Write What You Know

Write about the things that interest you. You're more likely to write well if you not only understand but also feel strongly about your topic. Your reader will know you've written from the heart.

What kinds of things do you know a lot about? Try writing about one of these ideas.

Do Your Research

For some types of writing, it's a good idea to do research before you begin writing. Facts and details will make your words more believable. Before you go to the library, write down everything you already know about your topic. You'll see how much more information you need to make your report strong. You might even talk to someone about your topic. Learning and thinking about another person's point of view can only make your writing better.

Stick to the Topic

It's important to think about ways to keep your writing centered on your topic. Decide what readers really need to know. If you're writing about your pet turtle, focus on what it looks like and give some details about how it acts and why you like it.

Rough Drafts

Now write a rough draft. Write as though you are telling a story to your friends, giving all the details but not worrying about how you sound. It's all right to have mistakes in a first draft. It's a good idea to write in the margins, cross out words, draw arrows, and move words around. A rough draft does not need to look neat. The important thing is to put your thoughts on paper. You can organize them better in later drafts.

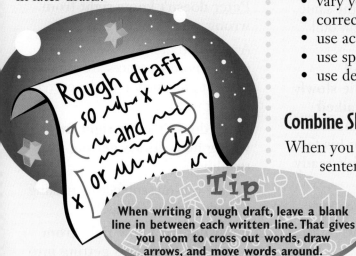

Reread and Edit

You don't need to be a perfect speller or to have mastered the rules of grammar to be a good writer. It is important, however, that you correct as many errors as possible before finishing a piece of writing. This may mean that you reread your work over and over until you're sure you've caught all your mistakes. In doing this, it's a good idea to make a checklist of things to look for. Then ask a friend or teacher to check your work for errors.

In editing your work, it's important to:

- combine short sentences
- vary your sentence beginnings
- correct sentence errors
- use active verbs
- use specific nouns
- use descriptive modifiers

Combine Short, Choppy Sentences

When you use a lot of short sentences, your writing may sound choppy and rough. Try to combine a few short sentences to balance your writing and ease the flow of words. Read the examples below and see how smoothly the sentences flow when some of them are combined.

Lisa walked home from school. She walked with her friend Angela. Lisa and Angela were great friends. They liked to play together. They never argued.

Now read the sentences when some of them are combined.

Lisa and her friend Angela walked home from school. They were great friends. They liked to play together and never argued.

Vary Your Sentence Beginnings

Make sure your sentences begin in different ways. If you start each sentence or paragraph in the same way, your writing may seem dull and boring.

Willie yawned loudly and stretched his arms. Willie slowly got out of bed. Willie walked down the hall to the bathroom. Willie splashed water on his face, brushed his teeth, and felt ready to start the day.

Begin with the same first sentence.

Willie yawned loudly and stretched his arms.

Use a pronoun and combine the two short sentences:

He slowly got out of bed and walked down the hall to the bathroom.

Begin the last sentence with a clause.

After splashing water on his face and brushing his teeth, Willie felt ready to start the day.

Correct Sentence Errors

Sentence fragments, run-on sentences, and rambling sentences are three of the most common errors people make in writing. They make your writing choppy and hard to read. Learn how to avoid these common errors.

A sentence fragment does not express a complete thought.

Doesn't know right from wrong. (The subject is missing.)

Fix the fragment by adding a subject.

Peter doesn't know right from wrong.

A run-on sentence occurs when two or more sentences are joined without punctuation or the correct linking word.

Peter doesn't know right from wrong he is always getting into trouble.

Fix the run-on sentence by making two separate sentences.

Peter doesn't know right from wrong. He is always getting into trouble.

A rambling sentence occurs when too many short sentences are joined with the word *and*.

Peter doesn't know right from wrong and he is always getting into trouble and he misses school a lot too and he also refuses to do his homework and he likes to act tougher than everyone else.

Fix the rambling sentence by getting rid of some of the *and*'s and making separate sentences.

Peter doesn't know right from wrong. He is always getting into trouble, and he misses school a lot. He also refuses to do his homework. He likes to act tougher than everyone else.

Use Active Verbs

Verbs are the force behind sentences. As action words, they drive your writing. Strong action verbs can make your writing come alive for the reader.

The ice skater <u>glided</u> across the ice like a swan. She <u>twirled</u> gracefully and <u>leaped</u> high in the air. The audience <u>erupted</u> in applause when she finished.

Use Specific Nouns

General nouns like *fruit, flowers,* and *dogs* do not always give a complete picture. Use words like *strawberry, roses,* and *Golden Retriever* to be more specific and paint a colorful picture for your reader.

Use Descriptive Adjectives and Adverbs

The right adjectives and adverbs can add spark to your writing and draw readers into your work. Read the examples below and see how the use of adjectives and adverbs add color to otherwise dull sentences.

Poor use of adjectives and adverbs: **The rain fell <u>hard</u> while the wind blew <u>loudly</u>.**

Better use of adjectives and adverbs: **The <u>harsh</u> rain fell on the <u>soggy</u> ground while the wind blew <u>fiercely</u>.**

Tip

Don't overuse modifiers. Too many adjectives and adverbs can make your writing sound forced and false.

You might want to use the checklist below to make sure you have looked for these things as you reread.

Rereading Checklist

_____ Did I write about something that interests me?

_____ Did I write clear and complete sentences?

_____ Did I write both short and long sentences?

_____ Did I begin my sentences in different ways?

Proofreading

In revising your work or that of others, it is helpful to use proofreading symbols. As you make corrections to the text, you can use standard proofreading symbols to show exactly what kinds of changes you want to make. Read on for some of the most common proofreading symbols.

Proofreading Symbols

⊙	add a period
#	add a space
cap or ≡	capitalization
l.c. or ⁄	make a lowercase letter
n.c.	not clear
∧	omission, add something
¶	paragraph
?	unclear
Sp.	spelling
⟋	switch the positions of words
✔	check this out
℮	take something out
w.c.	word choice

¶ Yesterday Mom and I went to the store⊙ ≡we looked for snacks for my sleepover party on Friday night. We bought pizza ∧rolls and ice cream for de∧sert. My M̸om even let me get sprinkles candy℮ to put on our ice cream. I can't wait until ∧my sleepover.

Proofreading Checklist

Use this checklist to edit and proofread your final draft:

Punctuation

____ Did I end each sentence with a punctuation mark?

____ Did I use commas in a series (*My mom, Seth, and I*)?

____ Did I use commas before conjunctions (*and, or, but*)?

____ Did I punctuate dialogue correctly?

Capitalization

____ Did I begin each sentence with a capital letter?

____ Did I capitalize nouns that name specific people, places, things, and ideas?

Spelling

____ Did I check for spelling, either with a dictionary or on a computer spell-checker?

Tip

Don't forget that a dictionary and computer spell-checker are excellent tools to help you correct spelling errors. But beware! Computer spell-checkers won't catch the use of the wrong homophone. For example:

I will <u>bee</u> home soon.

really should be

I will <u>be</u> home soon.

Spell check

Dictionary

Commonly Misused Words

Below is a list of commonly misused words. These words sound the same or similar or are often confused with each other. Read through each set of words and their meanings. Then read the examples. If you are ever unsure about which word to use, consult a dictionary.

accept, except
I <u>accept</u> your offer to work here.
I have everything I need <u>except</u> for the green paint.

a lot
Mike hopes to make <u>a lot</u> of money in his new job.

already, all ready
I <u>already</u> took my weekly spelling test.
I'm <u>all ready</u> to go to dinner.

bare, bear
It's too cold to walk around in <u>bare</u> feet.
A <u>bear</u> sleeps in winter.

blew, blue
The wind <u>blew</u> gently.
The sky was clear <u>blue</u>.

by, buy
The plane whizzed <u>by</u> overhead.
Alton wants to <u>buy</u> a new coat for winter.

can, may
<u>Can</u> Shane win the pie-eating contest?
<u>May</u> I go to the carnival on Saturday?

cent, scent, sent
A penny is worth one <u>cent</u>.
The flower shop had a strong <u>scent</u>.
My dad <u>sent</u> my mom flowers.

chose, choose
Antonia <u>chose</u> to walk home from school.
They often <u>choose</u> to walk home from school.

close, clothes
<u>Close</u> the door, please.
Grandpa has worn the same <u>clothes</u> since 1977.

creak, creek
Old and worn floors sometimes <u>creak</u> when you walk on them.
The water in the <u>creek</u> flows quietly.

dear, deer
I hold my friends <u>dear</u> to my heart.
<u>Deer</u> are shy animals.

desert, dessert	The <u>desert</u> is dry and hot. Rodrigo always saves room for <u>dessert</u>.
dew, do, due	I love the feel of morning <u>dew</u> on my bare feet. Bart forgot to <u>do</u> his chores last night. Homework is always <u>due</u> at the beginning of class.
doesn't, don't	Huang <u>doesn't</u> like boxing. I <u>don't</u>, either.
eye, I	I poked myself in the <u>eye</u>. <u>I</u> have perfect vision.
fewer, less	Hank has <u>fewer</u> baseball cards than Joseph. Hank has <u>less</u> time to collect baseball cards.
fir, fur	<u>Fir</u> trees are evergreen trees. Many people don't like the idea of <u>fur</u> coats.
for, four	I'm excited <u>for</u> you. Jamie's little brother is <u>four</u> years old.
good, well	Have a <u>good</u> day. Our team played <u>well</u>.
hare, hair	A <u>hare</u> looks like a big rabbit. Dad is losing his <u>hair</u> with age.
heal, heel	That cut should <u>heal</u> soon. Sammy injured the <u>heel</u> of his foot.
hear, here	It's hard to <u>hear</u> the TV when the buses go by outside. Most of the time it's quiet in <u>here</u>.
hi, high	Don't forget to say <u>hi</u> to the coach for me. The flag is flying <u>high</u>.
hole, whole	A bagel has a <u>hole</u> in the middle. I always eat the <u>whole</u> bagel for breakfast.
hour, our	Mom takes a yoga class for an <u>hour</u> on Wednesday nights. <u>Our</u> family believes that exercise is important.
its, it's	The cat licked <u>its</u> paws. <u>It's</u> a very cute kitten.

51

knew, new

Kim <u>knew</u> all of the answers on the game show.
She bought a <u>new</u> dress for the occasion.

knight, night

Fairy tales often involve a <u>knight</u> in shining armor.
The stars shine brightly at <u>night</u>.

knot, not

Sailors know how to make and undo every kind of <u>knot</u>.
I am <u>not</u> very good with my hands.

knows, nose

My teacher <u>knows</u> a lot about the planet Mars.
Margo has freckles on her <u>nose</u>.

lay, lie

<u>Lay</u> the pillow on the bed.
<u>Lie</u> down and take a nap.

lead, led

It's important to make sure there isn't any <u>lead</u> in the water.
The mayor <u>led</u> the city parade.

loose, lose

My shoelaces came <u>loose</u> in gym.
I thought for sure that I would <u>lose</u>.

mail, male

The <u>mail</u> is delivered six days a week.
A <u>male</u> is a man.

main, Maine, mane

My <u>main</u> concern is that I'll miss my flight.
The state of <u>Maine</u> is famous for its delicious blueberries.
A horse has a <u>mane</u> of hair on its neck.

meat, meet

Vegetarians don't eat <u>meat</u>.
My friends and I <u>meet</u> every Sunday morning for breakfast.

oar, or, ore

Use an <u>oar</u> to row the boat.
We can take a speedboat <u>or</u> a sailboat.
<u>Ore</u> is a mineral that contains metal.

one, won

Liza's family has <u>one</u> car.
Elizabeth <u>won</u> the race for class president.

pain, pane

I was in <u>pain</u> after the book fell on my foot.
The window <u>pane</u> needed to be washed.

pair, pare, pear

Ted wore his new <u>pair</u> of cowboy boots.
To <u>pare</u> an apple means to peel it.
I usually eat a juicy <u>pear</u> for dessert.

passed, past	Ramon had already <u>passed</u> several gas stations. It's best to think ahead and not dwell on the <u>past.</u>
peace, piece	Many politicians speak of working toward world <u>peace</u>. Joy asked for a small <u>piece</u> of pumpkin pie.
plain, plane	Jan wore a <u>plain</u> dress to her wedding. As a result of bad weather, the <u>plane</u> took off an hour late.
pore, pour, poor	A <u>pore</u> is a tiny opening in the skin. Would you <u>pour</u> the milk, please? I felt <u>poor</u> after I spent my allowance.
read, red	I <u>read</u> the book in just one sitting. Damien has bright <u>red</u> hair.
right, write	Is this the <u>right</u> place to sign up for the karate class? Did you <u>write</u> a thank-you letter to Grandpa?
road, rode, rowed	The <u>road</u> was dusty and rocky. We <u>rode</u> horses around the corral. Sumi <u>rowed</u> the boat to shore.
sea, see	Adrian has always liked the salty air by the <u>sea</u>. Alma can't <u>see</u> very well without her glasses.
seam, seem	The <u>seam</u> in Melvin's shirt was unraveling. He didn't <u>seem</u> to care, though.
sew, so, sow	My mom taught me how to <u>sew</u> when I was just ten years old. Her car had a flat tire, <u>so</u> she was late. A gardener must <u>sow</u> seeds to grow plants.
sit, set	May I <u>sit</u> down next to you? Latoya carefully <u>set</u> her tea on the glass table.
some, sum	Priya sold <u>some</u> of her old sweaters to earn extra money. The <u>sum</u> of 10 and 10 is 20.
son, sun	I'd like to have both a <u>son</u> and a daughter. The <u>sun</u> finally came out from behind the clouds.
stationery, stationary	Fiona writes letters on fancy <u>stationery</u>. My <u>stationary</u> bike doesn't go anywhere when I pedal.

tail, tale	The dog wagged its <u>tail</u> excitedly. Javier likes to tell <u>tales</u> about his family.
than, then	I'm taller <u>than</u> you. Let's go shopping and <u>then</u> go to lunch.
their, there, they're	Yvonne and her sister went to visit <u>their</u> grandparents. Juan likes to go over <u>there</u> because the kids have a lot of toys. I think <u>they're</u> nice people.
threw, through	The pitcher <u>threw</u> the ball hard and fast. The dog jumped <u>through</u> hoops at the circus.
to, too, two	Dad dislikes going <u>to</u> the dentist. I am <u>too</u> tired to cook dinner for the family tonight. Drake has <u>two</u> younger sisters.
waist, waste	Niles complains that his <u>waist</u> is getting too big. Pierre doesn't like to <u>waste</u> too much of his time.
wait, weight	Julio is impatient and refuses to <u>wait</u> for anyone. It's hard to lose <u>weight</u> if you don't exercise.
wear, where	Ruthie likes to <u>wear</u> large hoop earrings every day. Do you know <u>where</u> the Rocky Mountains are?
which, witch	<u>Which</u> dress should I wear to the concert? Zoe dressed as a <u>witch</u> for Halloween.
who's, whose	<u>Who's</u> going to take me to my swim meet? <u>Whose</u> goggles are these?
wood, would	The burning <u>wood</u> in the fireplace smelled good. <u>Would</u> you mind turning up the heat?
you're, your	<u>You're</u> going to get into trouble for skipping school. <u>Your</u> dad will be very upset.

Index